# Rage and Grief: A Healing Journey

Olivia Latham

Rage and Grief: A Healing Journey © 2024
Olivia Latham

All rights reserved.



Presentation by *BookLeaf Publishing*

Web: www.bookleafpub.com

E-mail: info@bookleafpub.com

ISBN: 9789360941659

First edition 2024

*For my father who told me I would never publish. Fuck you.*

# ACKNOWLEDGEMENT

Thanks to Gwen, who vetted almost every single piece in this, to Lauren and Evan, who gave me writing suggestions, encouragement, and constant reassurance: you guys really are the best. A huge thank you to Mom and Mac for being with me every step of the way and knowing the truth behind all these words. And, finally, to Rustam for encouraging my need to write.

# Sacrificial Lamb

We care not at all for
The sacrificial lamb meant to
Appease an angry god
We care only that
The danger is stopped, that
It is no longer our problem, that
What we love is safe

Gladly we drag the knife
Brutally 'cross its throat
Rejoicing it is not us, we
Ignore its piteous screams
Taking its bloody carcass
From the far bloodier altar
To throw on a pile of corpses

Never once do we think
But what of the lamb?
What of the innocence shed?
What of the weeping mother?
Forever mourning what's taken
Lost and lonely for purity
Waiting on the return of her
Missing child, whole and well

We think only of the god who's
Locked away, temporarily sated
No longer hunting our children
Sacrifice one for the many, the
Bodies of the one soon rise high
*What safety we can find in*
*these dead-eyed violent rituals.*

We pray frantically, hoping prayer
Shall aid in our salvation (*escape*)
But His hunger never truly rests
It gnaws at His belly, discontent
He would eat the whole world if
We allowed it, if we stopped our
Grim offerings (*so we tell ourselves*)

Perhaps one day, we shall find the perfect lamb
to slake His endless lust
Perhaps, one day, the bodies will stop gathering

# Father Is a Monster

I click off the television and
Ponder
Yet another case of a father
Killing his daughter
Wonder at the how and why
And who let it get that far?
Then I wonder what should I say
Or do?
It seems the only thing is
Nothing

So I live my life like there's
Nothin' wrong
All la di da, singin' a song
Try to drown out and pull
Back
And I remind myself
Don't let it sink in too deep
Don't let it consume
Remember that it's all over
For now

Now I lay me down to sleep
Pillow soft, so soft and sweet
But my head is too full

So close to bursting like a dam
Filled with all the sorrow and pain
Of the day, week, month, year
Of the many, many years
And so I go to sleep
Troubled thoughts turned to
Troubled dreams

i walk down the street of
a city
and pass by a fair,
a crowd draws me in
<u>Helplessly</u>
but for all its size it was
<u>Silent.</u>
i am no fish to swim upstream
so i go in and enter the teeming
swarm

a vendor greets us, cold as
stone
and bids us follow to his booth
where we come upon his work
my skin prickles at the utter
<u>Quiet</u> of the crowd
i raise my hand to ask the name
of the centerpiece displayed
icily, condescendingly, the vendor
reprimanded me

<u>Your Father Is a Monster.</u>

the painting shows
a little girl, face/cheeks
<u>Bruised</u>
with father's large fingers
gripping hard onto his small
<u>Daughter</u>.
shadows stretch behind him
obscuring him in violence
as i look, i see
an older woman, head turned away
a glass of milk spilled
perhaps by the careless hands of a
child,
the <u>Rage</u> becomes even more
a <u>Parent</u>

i step forward to <u>Take It In</u>
i see the girl's eyes plead
staring right at the crowd
and i know them for
<u>My Own</u>
i start to yell
to scream
to stop it
to stop this
violent voyeurism, this
<u>Consumption</u>

but the crowd remains silent
impassive
in the face of my despair
and i realize they cannot, will not
<u>Help</u>
they have condemned <u>Me</u>/her
with their inaction,
their awful empty eyes
just stare
With a start I awaken to
Darkness

# Fat

7

One day, I told Dad I was depressed. He said, "No, you aren't. You're just fat."

# Because I Love You

Still I hear his voice in my head
Taunting me, ridiculing loudly
My every choice
My every love
My every fault
Leaving me as scattered glass
And mocking my inability
To safely gather the pieces
Blood pouring from grasping hands
No sound may pass trembling lips
*I'm only doing this because I love you*
Violence exhaled in every breath
And I am left inhaling fumes
Choking on spewed toxins
But don't complain
Never complain
Be grateful I'm allowed to breathe
At all
Suppress the fury in my lungs
No hacking coughs to hint at my rage
I hunger for clean air
Growing twisted under his care and
Adapted to his pollution
It is a shock when finally the air
Starts to clear

Yet the damage remains
And I am left to wonder
Is it too late
Am I truly my father's daughter?

# Summer Day

Tiny hands play with long willow branches
Tearing off a length carelessly
Stripping the leaves 'til bare
Weaving it around itself till a crown is made
Unaware of the hurt caused, caring only
That the thing be made
The air thickly perfumed with gardenias
And the happy shrieks of children
Leaving behind a dark house, looking for the
next adventure
That hazy summer day, that endless afternoon
A
moment
      once
stretched

now relegated to mere memory
But that house was dark for a reason
No amount of shrieking children
Could cover the horror inside
That hazy summer day lost within
A string of bitter winter months
And overshadowed by an angry man
Who would devour the whole world
If only we allowed

# Destruction (of Public Property)

Boys will be boys and girls grow up faster. It's locker room talk, it can't hurt anyone. It's your word against his. You're overreacting. You asked for it, you shouldn't have drank/smoked. Your skirt was too short, your makeup too slutty. Keep quiet, you can't ruin his career or reputation. He made one stupid mistake. Your eyes said yes, your mouth said no. It's too hard for them to understand. You can't pass out on the floor, don't go to the bathroom without a friend. Don't stay out too late, don't walk home alone. Lock your doors as soon as you get to your car. They can grab you by the pussy, just don't fight back. Don't you know, you, as public property, belong to everyone?

# Whose Body Is It Anyways?

My body is not my own
I am a tenant waiting for the landlord
To evict me from my home

Husband or fetus they have
More claim, a better stake
On the body I've always inhabited

Through tearful eyes I say I do
A gun pointed to my head
There's no one to stop my rape

Fucked and bred like an animal
It doesn't matter if this thing kills me
There's no harm, so long as it's born

With rage in my eyes, I beg
For what, I do not yet know
I have known nothing else than this

This wretched, gross object-ness
Not once have I ever been a person
Just property paraded before others

My consumption is matter of course

Not once will you think twice
Beyond the fruit of my womb (Blessed Be)

13

I'd rather be put down as a dog
Hunted for sport, bullet in my brain
Than kept penned in as cattle

But my say never mattered much to you, did it?

# 8th Grade Crush

I knew it for a sin when I felt longing
At her touch upon my cheek
Her lips soft and sweet
Kissing away streaming tears
My stomach bloomed with heat
Awash in shame and confusion
I never realized trailing fingers
Could ignite such gentle burning
That night is when I started praying
To be as I was, ignorant and innocent
Offering bargains in exchange
If it would just go away
*Please, I'll do anything, I swear*
Silence was my only answer and
My yearning grew alongside
My endless recriminations
I recognized the shape of me
As an abomination in the eyes of God
Self-hatred became an oft-worn coat
Drawn tight and much belov'd
Its fabric tattered and worn
Providing little protection and no warmth
Yet it was all I deserved
This constant imposed deprivation
My ascetic ways the only possible path

To eternal grace

So I was made to believe

# For Love (of a Man)

Swallow me whole
Let not one morsel slip past
Your cherry sweet lips
I wish to be taken by your
Darkness,
I wish for mine
To stretch out its loving arms
Towards you(rs)
So we may meet in awful
Desire
Tear me apart
Nothing need remain
Save my beating heart
Clutched tight in strong
Hands, I
See the hunger in your eyes, feel
The force of my snapping neck
The grip on my hair,
Hear the raggedness of breathing
Unchecked
Spend yourself in me
Show me what it is
To be the fire in a tinder
Dry forest, flames raging
Between

I don't care if I am burned
To ash floating on the breeze, the
Specks spread to all four corners, isn't this
How love was always meant
To be?

In your consumption, you have been cleansed
In your burning, purified of the sin of your birth
In your destruction, became holy
May it ever be so for the love of a man
Amen

# Bleed Out

My love is a thorn clutched tight to
My breast
The tip lightly puncturing the aching muscle
Of my beating heart
I caress it gently, hoping kindness will soften it
That my tenderness be seen and known
That my hard-fought-for goodness
Will get it to love me in turn
Instead
          it
              burrows
Seeking shelter yet returning none
Craving the warmth of my blood
While driving ice into my veins
Promising to bloom if only I'd water it thus
Should I but pluck this thorn, the pain would end
But oh gods I should also bleed out

# Worthy Offerings

Nobody wants me
They want the things I represent
Not the whole, not the truth
Not the shivering, vicious thing
Backed into a corner, looking for any kind of
Escape

They want my body
The lush curves promising pleasure
The mouth ripe for stolen kisses
The hair soft and full, inviting buried hands
The eyes drawing them in, begging for my
Conquest

I am the object, the fantasy
As soon as I become more, a person
They pull away, attempt to domesticate me
Building walls that move ever closer
I am trapped, diminished, a shadow of
Myself

They tell me what I am
What I'm not, what I feel, how to act
A doll to play with, they move my limbs in
Reckless abandon, it's a shock when finally

I break, no longer pliant, no longer docile, I am
All rage

Still they want gifted pieces
Served to them on silver platters, yet
Wonder at the lack of worthy offerings
Why I clutch at the remaining scraps
They hate the thing I've become, the creature
They shaped

But can they not see? I am the idol they made
with their own two hands

# Why Don't You Sing Anymore?

I never wrote when I was with her
The words would not come from
My singing tongue
She forbade its use, stating it
Hurt her sensitive ears
Then complained at my silence
For it offended just as much

# January 3rd

I think of my ex-lover
Her nervous fingers
Reaching
Reaching
Reaching
Inside my chest
To try and possess what
I would have given
Freely
Her frost overtaking
The iciness in my veins
Echoes the iciness of
Chill winter air
Grey and
Bitter and
Dead
She and her birth month are
Well-matched
In all the ways we never were
To celebrate her birth, I eat a
Spoonful of peanut butter
Satisfaction finally mine
My mouth now her poison
The spring to her winter
All trace of her

Erased
With the languid waking of
Fallow earth

# Longing, Haunted Thing

This craving, this longing, haunted thing
Deep within, deep beneath
Crawling, reaching, clawing towards the sun
Taking gasping lungfuls of air
Go back from whence you came
The shadows of the earth beckon you
Bid you return
Return to their embrace, return to the silence
You are not wanted here
This thing that you are and have been
What good does it do?
It kills you what lies under the skin
Itching, lurking, driving you forward
How dare you answer its call?
Better that your hips stay unblemished
Better that your hands stay clean
Better that the darkness inside stay unseen
This monster longs to be free
Don't open that prison, don't let it creep
Towards the light
It destroys you being caged
But for all concerned
It is better that
This craving, this longing, haunted thing
Slumber still

# A Body that Hates Me

I say I hate my body
But that sounds so trivial, so banal
After all, doesn't everyone hate their body?
Isn't everyone critical of the things it does?
The way it sags, the way it crinkles, how it
bends
But that isn't what I mean when I say I hate my
body
I don't mean I wish I could slice myself into tiny
ribbons to create a version more pleasing
One that is small and palatable, easily slid down
the gullet
As a particularly tasty *amuse-bouche*
When I say I hate my body
I mean
That my body is an utter failure
That it refuses to function unassisted
That I can become reality-untethered in the blink
of an eye
That I can't seem to hold my shape, my bones
twisting serpentine, damaging chiffon skin
That my body is also my tomb
Every morning I count out
1, 2, 3, 4, 5 pills to get me through the day
1 to clear sludge from my mind

2 to quiet my pitter-patter heart
1 to fight the demons
Yet another to alchemize oxygen from air
My body is my enemy and it requires constant
vigilance
Ready to attack at the slightest provocation
A cornered, wounded animal
And me, myself, and I its prime target
No room for peace between us and I am
reminded that
I am my body and my body is me
What a thing to be so bound to something so
cruel
Yet even with all its magnificent viciousness
I wish I knew how to love a body that hates me
back

# May the Crows Feast

I know what it is to die
To be inside my body quietly rotting
Watching the world around me move on
While I lay in envy
Mourning the days when I was alive
But then
I make my peace with it
With the dark, with the silence
With the pain of my immovable bones
No prayer shall heal, no saint shall save
No act of god shall raise them from this dirt
It is me in this shallow grave known as
My Body
And I have been left for the maggots
I hope the crows peck out my eyes
So they, at least, may eat
Perhaps then I shall live again through them
And see as one who is
Free

# Rot

Only let me rot here with you
at the end of all things, in the
screaming wild dark

Limbs intertwined, together
we decay in the soft, fallow
earth for the ages

# One Day, Today

One day

        I resolved to be greedy for life
     To scoop it up with my own two hands
   And watch it spill between them rapidly
  Splashing down my body, messy and cold
      The shock bringing clarity

One day

       I decided I didn't want to die
  That I didn't want to just disappear gently
  Into that quiet dark, no whimper to mark
   My inevitable end without first living
     Without first tasting all I can

One day

      I found pleasure to be more holy
    Than our blind obeisance to pain
  Its altar choked with rich offerings yet
    Absent is the god which rules
   *Oh Father, art thou really in heaven?*

One day

     I allowed love to be a feast
  And let loose the leash of my gluttony
    My hunger pangs at last soothed
  Shame abandoned (finally) as useless
     No longer shall I starve

One day

I wanted to fuck
To worship the primal of my body
Allowing others to glory in my delights
Nectar dripping from open mouths and
Shared between silken tongues

And what of today, you may ask
Well today, today I revel in it all with
bacchanalian glee